CENSORSHIP

How Does It Conflict with Freedom?

Richard Steins

Twenty-First Century Books

A Division of Henry Holt and Co
New York

Twenty-First Century Books
A division of Henry Holt and Company, Inc.
115 West 18th Street
New York, New York 10011

Henry Holt® and colophon are registered trademarks of Henry Holt and
Company, Inc.
Publishers since 1866

Published in Canada by Fitzhenry & Whiteside Ltd.
195 Allstate Parkway, Markham, Ontario L3R 4T8

Printed in the United States of America

Created and produced in association with Blackbirch Graphics, Inc.

Library of Congress Cataloging-in-Publication Data

Steins, Richard.
    Censorship : How does it conflict with freedom? / Richard Steins.
    — 1st ed.
        p.   cm. — (Issues of our time)
    Includes bibliographical references and index.
    ISBN 0-8050-3879-5
    1. Censorship—United States—Juvenile literature. 2. Freedom of speech—United
States—Juvenile literature. 3. Freedom of the press—United States—Juvenile
literature. [1. Censorship. 2. Freedom of speech. 3. Freedom of the press.]
    I. Title. II. Series.
    Z658.U5S74   1995
    363.3'1'0973—dc20   94-41761
                                                                                       CIP
                                                                                        AC

Contents

▪ ▪ ▪ ▪ ▪ ▪

1

·······

Freedoms in a Free Society

Among the many freedoms we enjoy in the United States are free speech and a free press. The First Amendment to the U.S. Constitution, adopted in 1791, states in part that "Congress shall make no law...abridging the freedom of speech, or of the press...." But what exactly does that mean? May we say or write anything we wish, regardless of the consequences?

Almost every American would say that he or she is against censorship—that is, the limiting or the prevention of free speech and a free press by individuals, groups, or the government. But some people also believe that there should be limitations on the freedoms found in the First

The founders of the United States believed that a free society needed basic rights protected by the Constitution. They added the First Amendment to ensure that Americans would have free speech, a free press, and freedom of religion.

Amendment. They would argue, for example, that people do not have the right to advocate violence or to preach hatred. Others believe, however, that the First Amendment completely protects anyone's right to speak or write whatever he or she wishes, even if those opinions are unpopular with the majority of the people.

The debate over how much freedom we should have versus how many limitations there should be on our freedoms has been going on since the signing of the Constitution in 1787. It continues to this day.

Burning a National Symbol

In 1984, a young man committed an act that was illegal under Texas state law and that most Americans thought should be punished. When the Republican National Convention met in Dallas, Texas, that summer to renominate President Ronald Reagan for a second term, a man named Gregory Johnson held a rally outside the convention hall to protest the president's policies. After a march through the streets with a number of his supporters, Johnson set fire to an American flag while the crowd chanted: "America, the red, the white, and blue, we spit on you."

Johnson was immediately arrested and convicted for both abusing and destroying an American flag, which was illegal under Texas law. Most Americans consider the flag to be a revered symbol of our nation and of the sacrifices that people have made to defend our freedom. The Texas law was very clear, and Johnson was convicted of violating it.

He appealed his conviction to the Texas Court of Criminal Appeals on the grounds that burning the flag was a form of political speech and was therefore protected under the First Amendment. That court agreed and threw out his conviction. The state of Texas then decided to take the case to the highest court in the country—the U.S. Supreme Court—which would decide if Johnson's conduct was a form of free speech guaranteed by the Constitution.

In 1989, five years after the incident in Dallas, the Supreme Court gave a verdict in the case of *Texas v. Johnson*. The Court ruled that "if there is a bedrock principle underlying the First Amendment, it is that the government may not prohibit the expression of an idea simply because society itself finds the idea

Gregory Johnson celebrated the Supreme Court's decision by burning a flag at a victory rally in New York City's Tompkins Square Park.

itself offensive or disagreeable." Johnson's act was found to be protected speech under the First Amendment, and the law in Texas and in forty-seven other states was declared unconstitutional.

People were outraged, and some members of Congress tried to pass a constitutional amendment making it a federal crime to abuse or destroy an American flag. The effort failed and the controversy died down.

Why Have Free Speech and a Free Press?

In the 1780s, shortly after America became independent, it was not uncommon in Europe for opponents of governments to be harassed and jailed, and for their newspapers and other publications to be censored by the government or even shut down.

The founders of the United States believed that a free society could not survive unless basic freedoms were assured. They did not want European habits to damage the new country. In addition, they believed that a democratic society in which people govern themselves needs freedom of information and an exchange of ideas in order for people to make wise decisions. For this reason, they specifically added the First Amendment to the Constitution; it spelled out a number of freedoms, including free speech, a free press, and freedom of religion.

As the founders of our nation clearly understood, people must have the right to express ideas, even ones that everyone else might disagree with. Nonetheless, Americans have argued since then about what the First Amendment means and how it should be applied.

Listening to People
We Disagree With
Voltaire, a French philosopher, poet, and champion of free thought said, "I disapprove of what you say, but will defend to the death your right to say it."

It is sometimes difficult to listen to people we disagree with. It is even more difficult when we not only disagree, but believe the other person has opinions that are hurtful to others.

Suppose, for example, that someone in your class believes that all illegal immigrants should be forced to leave the United States. You, on the other hand, believe that the United States should be open to all people who want to move here in order to improve their lives—even if they have entered the country without permission.

The other person is expressing a point of view you disagree with. But what if that person uses harsh words or racial slurs while making his or her arguments? Do you think that person should be allowed to say such things, especially since they are

Voltaire, an eighteenth-century French philosopher, strongly supported freedom of speech and fought to secure that right for all.

comments that might offend a person or hurt someone's feelings? Does free speech, which is one of
our treasured freedoms dating back to the founding
of our country, include the right to insult someone?
Or use bad language? Or to cause trouble in general? How far does our freedom of speech allow
us to go?

There are no easy answers to these questions.
For example, if you say in public that you strongly
disagree with the immigration policies of our government, you are exercising your right to express
your political point of view. This freedom is protected under our Constitution. And if you say in
public, "I think all illegal immigrants should be
expelled," you have expressed a harsh point of
view, but it is still your right to say it.

You may even do certain things that most Americans find completely wrong—like burning the
American flag or making critical remarks in public
about one particular group or another. This kind of
free expression may also be allowed under our
Constitution. However, if you say, "I think we
should get a mob together now and beat up all illegal immigrants," you could be in trouble. Your city
or state may have specific laws against encouraging
a mob to riot. And these laws may be constitutional—that is, they do not violate the spirit of the
Constitution. Therefore, expressing an unpopular

The First Amendment

Congress shall make no law respecting an establishment of religion, or prohibiting the free exercise thereof; or abridging the freedom of speech, or of the press; or the right of the people peaceably to assemble, and to petition the Government for a redress of grievances.

idea is not by itself forbidden; but the goal of the expression (starting a riot) might be.

Freedom of speech means that we all have the right to express our views, as long as we do not violate the Constitution in the process. The freedom to express our points of view—no matter how unpopular—also means that we may have an interest in listening to others, even people we disagree with, so that others will listen to us. Our opinions and points of view are strengthened when we have free speech, because we learn of the ideas of others. Benjamin Franklin said, "Without freedom of thought, there can be no such thing as wisdom; and no such thing as public liberty, without freedom of speech."

The great challenge to our democracy is to decide which kinds of free speech should be protected—and how we should protect them.

2

The First Amendment, the Government, and the Supreme Court

Although the framers of the Constitution made sure that free speech and a free press were among the first rights guaranteed to Americans, the U.S. government, during its more than 200-year history, has often attempted to limit those freedoms. The First Amendment is a very short statement. Its meaning and how it should be applied have been interpreted in different ways over the course of our nation's history.

In the 1800s, for example, most people believed that freedom of the press meant only that the government could not prevent something from being published *before* it came out. This

An argument is brought before the Supreme Court in 1910. For more than 200 years, constitutional questions of free speech, freedom of religion, and a free press have been ultimately decided by the Court.

was known as *prior restraint*—that is, stopping publication of a book, newspaper, or article before it comes into print. Under this limited view of the First Amendment, anyone has the right to publish something, but once it is in print, the government has the right to censor it.

The founders of the country accepted this view. In 1798, Congress passed the Sedition Act, a law that made it a crime to "utter false, scandalous, and malicious" statements about the federal government. The purpose of this law was to silence and imprison anyone who criticized the government. But when the government tried to prosecute people for violating the law, the public reacted against it. In 1800, President Thomas Jefferson pardoned all those who had been convicted under the act. The law expired in 1801 and it was not renewed.

During the Civil War (1861–1865), President Abraham Lincoln occasionally imprisoned some opponents of the war and shut down newspapers advocating rebellion. This form of government censorship was justified, said Lincoln, because the life of the nation was in grave danger. Twelve states had seceded from the Union and were in armed rebellion against the government. Under these circumstances, the president was acting to protect the nation during an emergency in his role as commander in chief of the armed forces.

President Lincoln enforced censorship during the Civil War because he felt the security of the nation was endangered by the freedom of the press.

Protected Free Speech
and Free Press Issues of free speech and a free press, like all major constitutional questions, eventually are decided by the Supreme Court. And the Court must set standards that define whether or not there should be any limits to how extensive free speech and a free press are in our society.

In America's early years, it was believed that the First Amendment was a *federal* protection; that is, it protected free speech and the press from interference by the federal government only and *not* by the state governments. As a result, very few cases involving issues of free speech and a free press came before the Supreme Court. States often passed laws limiting the freedom of speech and the press, but almost none of them were challenged before the Supreme Court.

This changed in 1925 in a case called *Gitlow v. New York*. The *Gitlow* decision was a revolutionary case in U.S. history. Benjamin Gitlow was a member of the Socialist party in New York State and the manager of a Socialist newspaper called *Revolutionary Age*. In 1919, he was convicted of violating a state law against "criminal anarchy." The New York State government claimed that the newspaper advocated the violent overthrow of the government.

When the case reached the Court in 1925, it ruled that the First Amendment applied to *state laws* as

In 1925, the Supreme Court decided that the guarantees of the First Amendment were more powerful than the state law and proclaimed Gitlow (above) innocent.

well. Justice Edward T. Sanford wrote, "We may and do assume that freedom of speech and of the press—which are protected by the 1st Amendment from abridgement by Congress—are among the fundamental personal rights and 'liberties' protected...from impairment by the states." The *Gitlow* case was a major expansion of the rights found in the First Amendment.

But did that mean that a person could actually advocate the overthrow of the government and go unpunished? Six years earlier, the Court addressed that question in *Schenck v. the United States*. In 1917, Charles T. Schenck was arrested for resisting the draft and distributing antidraft leaflets. At the time, America was fighting in World War I, and Congress had passed the Espionage Act of 1917, which made it illegal to resist the draft. The Court upheld the law, finding that in times of national danger the government has a right to protect the nation. At the same time, however, what is known as "clear and present danger" was created. Under these guidelines, the government would have to prove there was a clear and present danger to the nation for limitations on freedom to be allowed.

In 1969, this rule was expanded further when the Court ruled that only someone who advocates immediate, violent, and illegal action may be subject to criminal prosecution. Even so, the Court has often protected controversial actions that may seem violent. For example, in a 1992 case called *R.A.V. v. the City of St. Paul, Minnesota,* the Court ruled that a city law making it a crime to draw a Nazi swastika on public property violated the First Amendment as it punished a certain kind of speech based on its content. In the twentieth century, the Supreme Court has demonstrated the high value it places on First Amendment rights, especially the right to speak and publish unpopular political opinions.

Speech and Written Material Not Protected by the First Amendment

While expanding First Amendment rights concerning political speech and publishing, the Supreme Court has also defined four kinds of speech and written material that are *not* protected by the First Amendment.

Obscenity. What is obscenity? Most people do not agree. Some are offended by four-letter words in speech or print, while others are not. Some people feel that pictures showing sexual situations should be allowed to be published, while others believe that such material is not protected by a free press.

The Court has never been able to define exactly what is obscene. But it has tried to establish guidelines. In the 1973 case of *Miller v. California*, the

Because obscenity has not been clearly defined by the Court, states have made their own rules. Pornographic shops, for example, are allowed in some states and not in others.

Court established three tests for obscenity—(1) whether the average person, applying local community standards, would find something taken as whole to be obscene; (2) whether something depicts sexual conduct in an offensive way that is against local laws; and (3) whether something lacks "serious literary, artistic, political, and scientific value."

The Court's vagueness about what obscenity is has allowed state and local governments to enact a range of different laws defining it. All states ban pornographic material that exploits children. But some state and local governments allow bookstores to sell pornography, while others prohibit it. And the federal government has the power to prohibit indecent or obscene language from being spoken on the radio, television, or electronic media.

Libel and Slander. Libel is false or damaging information about someone's character and reputation, that appears in print or on television. Slander is speech that damages a person's character and reputation. State laws prohibit libel and slander, but the Court has tried to establish a balance so that libel and slander laws do not limit free speech and press.

In the 1988 *Hustler Magazine v. Falwell* case, the Court reversed a decision that had awarded the Reverend Jerry Falwell $200,000 for "emotional distress" over a cartoon about him that appeared in the sex-oriented magazine. The Court said that the cartoon was not presented as "fact," but only as a mockery of the minister, a spokesperson for politically conservative causes.

The *Hustler Magazine* case made it more difficult for well-known people to successfully sue for libel or slander. Libel and slander laws remain on the books in all states, but libel and slander are not protected by the guarantees of the First Amendment.

Fighting Words. "Fighting words" is the term used by the Supreme Court to describe speech that deliberately tries to incite violence. The term was first used in 1942, in a case called *Chaplinsky v.*

Libel, although protected by state laws, is not protected by the First Amendment. The Supreme Court ruled against Jerry Falwell in his 1988 case.

New Hampshire. In that case, the Court upheld the conviction of a man named Chaplinsky for calling a police officer "a goddamed racketeer." Such speech, said the Court, could be called "fighting words," likely to incite violence, and therefore was not protected by the First Amendment.

Commercial Speech. Commercial speech, or advertising, has for many years been considered unprotected speech. The government has a strong interest in regulating advertising—for example, to protect consumers from false claims and lies. Therefore, the Supreme Court has allowed commercial speech to fall outside the protection of the First Amendment and to be regulated by the federal government and the states.

A Continuing Debate
Within Government
As we have seen, the First Amendment guarantees are freedoms that are continually being examined and defined in changing situations. The Supreme Court has been very protective of free speech and a free press when it comes to political expression. In other areas, such as obscenity and libel, it has given less precise guidelines.

The federal and state governments continue to struggle with issues that relate to freedom of speech and the press.

Daniel Ellsberg: Hero or Lawbreaker?

Dr. Daniel Ellsberg worked in the Department of Defense in the early 1970s. One of his projects was a top-secret report on the history of U.S. involvement in the Vietnam War. The more Ellsberg worked, the more upset he became. He believed that the government had deceived Americans about the reasons for our involvement in Vietnam and had lied about every aspect of the conflict.

Even though the report was top secret (meaning only the highest ranking members of government could read it), Ellsberg decided to copy it and give it to the press.

On June 13, 1971, the *New York Times* and the *Washington Post* published portions of the report, which became known popularly as the "Pentagon Papers." President Richard Nixon was so angry that these documents had been "leaked" to the press that he ordered the Department of Justice to block publication of additional parts of the report.

The government got a court order forcing the *New York Times* to stop publication until the Supreme Court could rule. Two weeks later, the Court ruled that the government could not stop publication of the "Pentagon Papers," even though they had been stolen and leaked to the press. The Court stated that stopping publication would be "prior restraint," a violation of the First Amendment.

The Justice Department arrested Ellsberg for espionage, but his case was dismissed before trial because of illegal government actions. The Nixon administration was mad and hired a group known as the "Plumbers" to break into Ellsberg's psychiatrist's office in search of damaging information. This illegal action was one factor in the downfall of the Nixon administration in 1974.

Was Ellsberg a hero by letting the American people know about the actions of their government? Or was he simply a lawbreaker? The Supreme Court recognized the constitutional issue of prior restraint, but also agreed that Ellsberg had probably broken the law. Ellsberg never had to face the charge of espionage because the government itself had committed crimes in prosecuting him.

Freedom of the press was questioned when Daniel Ellsberg turned over classified government information to the news media.

Censorship of Speech

There have been many incidents that have occurred in the United States in recent years that have tested the limits of free-speech rights in our society. The following events offer a few examples:

• A group of American Nazis holds a march and rally in a Chicago suburb and preaches hatred against all African-Americans and Jews.

• A group of noisy protesters camps out every day in front of a women's clinic in Florida, shouting that abortion is murder and sometimes blocking access to the clinic.

• An African-American professor at a large university gives a speech in New York in which he blames Jews for much of the oppression of African-American people in America.

Whether you are for or against any controversial issue, freedom of speech guarantees your right to speak out. Here, Operation Rescue, an antiabortion group, holds a demonstration.

Should people be allowed to say anything in public, even if it is hurtful? Should groups be allowed to have demonstrations that may prevent others from exercising their rights? Should students be allowed to express their political views in school?

Free Speech Versus Hate Speech

The American Nazi party models itself after the German Nazis. This highly vocal group preaches hatred of all Jews and African-Americans. In 1977, they chose to hold a march in Skokie, Illinois, a suburb of Chicago with a large Jewish population. They picked Skokie in order to upset its Jewish members, many of whom had survived the Holocaust in Europe during World War II. (The Holocaust was a horrible event in world history, during which the Nazi party systematically murdered more than six million Jews.)

The village of Skokie outlawed the rally. But the Nazis went to court to challenge the ban, and in the end, the Supreme Court upheld their right under the First Amendment to hold

The guarantees of the First Amendment have a price. Here, the National Socialist (Nazi) Party of America holds a hate march in St. Louis. These marches are protected by the First Amendment.

their rally, even though it would upset many people. The Court said that "anticipation of a hostile audience could not justify...prior restraint." It also made it clear that the police had to protect the people participating in the rally. The meeting was held under tight police supervision and it ended without incident.

The Skokie case upset many people who believed that pure hate speech should not be protected by the First Amendment. The Supreme Court, however, once again upheld the right of a group to express an opinion publicly, no matter how unpopular.

Peaceful Protest

Versus Harassment The right of a woman to have an abortion in the United States is generally protected by the 1973 Supreme Court decision *Roe v. Wade*. Despite the law, however, people opposed to abortion have fought to reverse the *Roe* decision and to outlaw abortion.

One of the most frequently used tactics of the antiabortion movement is to protest in front of any facility that offers abortion services. Some antiabortion groups, such as Operation Rescue, have tried to block access to clinics by staging sit-ins at clinic entrances. They claim that their protest is peaceful and nonviolent, although it does prevent women from entering the clinics.

Dr. John Britton, an abortion doctor in Pensacola, Florida, was killed in July 1994. Although antiabortion groups have been guaranteed freedom of speech, violent acts have caused the Supreme Court to place restrictions on those rights.

Opponents of Operation Rescue argued that the group was not protesting peacefully, but was harassing women and conspiring to prevent them from exercising their lawful right to have an abortion. In 1991, the Supreme Court ruled that a federal law against conspiracies to deny people their civil rights could *not* be used against protesters who blocked abortion clinics. In 1994, however, the Court ruled that a law prohibiting racketeering (creating a social clamor using intimidation) *could* be used against them. Members of Operation Rescue complained that their First Amendment rights to free speech were being denied. While not banning the protests outright, the Court ruled that they could take place no closer than forty feet from the clinic entrances.

Academic Freedom or Racebaiting?

Dr. Leonard Jeffries is a professor at the City University of New York and chair of its African Studies Department. In 1991, he made a public speech stating that American Jews were partially responsible for oppressing African-Americans.

His speech created an uproar, and many called for Jeffries to resign. When he refused, he was removed by the university. Jeffries went to court, demanding he be reinstated. The court agreed, on the basis that he had not been denied his position for failing to do his job, but for expressing unpopular views. But in November 1994, the Supreme Court told the lower court to reconsider its ruling.

Those who disagreed with the lower court felt Jeffries was racist and that, as a professor paid by taxpayers, he had an obligation to observe standards that apply to people in public life. A university, they argued, should not be a shelter for racism.

Jeffries's case came at a time when relations between African-Americans and Jews in America were strained. Louis Farrakhan, the leader of the Muslim group Nation of Islam, had been making comments that people found offensive. Farrakhan made several speeches calling white people "devils" and attacking Jews. Some called him a racebaiter and others said he had a right to express his views under the code of academic freedom.

Leonard Jeffries challenged the idea that every person has the right to express their opinion, no matter how unpopular it is.

Censorship in the Military: Freedom to Know
Versus National Security

In 1991, Cable Network News (CNN) reports on the Gulf War were censored by both the American and the Iraqi military.

Censorship of information about military activities has a long history in the United States, especially during wartime. In World War II (1939–1945), the government kept a tight lid on casualty figures and on future battle plans. Newspapers reported on events *after* they occurred, not before.

Despite the government's reasons for using censorship in wartime, the press—and in more recent times, TV reporters—has never been happy about it. The issue arose again in 1991, during the Persian Gulf War.

When the war began, the Department of Defense established the rules that TV reporters would have to follow while covering the conflict. All "live" interviews had to be shown to military censors before being broadcast to make sure they did not endanger the security of American forces. But the rule that bothered reporters the most was the use of "pools." Instead of allowing all reporters and their camera crews to travel anywhere they wanted, the military required that they travel in pools. TV crews had to designate certain reporters to get a story. Each pool was also accompanied by a military "guide."

TV reporters felt the pools were designed to keep them from discovering information. Also, the guide might prevent them from asking certain kinds of questions and could intervene and stop the interview in the name of "national security."

The TV networks complained loudly, but the war was over quickly and the issue was never tested. Most TV reporters felt the purpose of the restrictions was not just to protect the security of the troops. They believed the government did not want reporters discovering things that were not going well. Any TV reporter who tried to get a story outside of the pool faced having his or her credentials taken away by the military.

The American public supported restrictions on TV news, and on the press in general, during the Gulf War. A poll taken just before the war began revealed that 88 percent believed censorship was necessary under the circumstances. The issue, however, is complex. The public has a right to know about decisions that affect the lives of soldiers. The soldiers also have a right to be protected as much as possible as they risk their lives for their country.

Teenagers and Free Speech

As minors, do teenagers have a constitutional right to express their points of view?

This question was tested during the 1960s, when the United States was involved in the war in Vietnam. Teenagers at a high school in Des Moines, Iowa, protested American involvement in the war by wearing black armbands. School officials refused to allow the protest, saying it would disrupt the classroom. Two students, John and Mary Beth Tinker, took their case to court, saying they had been denied their First Amendment rights. The students said the wearing of armbands was symbolic speech that had been censored.

The case went to the Supreme Court where the justices decided in favor of the students. The Court said it was a form of free speech. School officials retained the right to ban disruptive protests, but the armbands did not disturb the school's atmosphere.

John and Mary Beth Tinker display the armbands the Supreme Court ruled they were allowed to wear, in the name of "symbolic speech."

One of the roots of our democracy is the right of all people to express their points of view, even if those views are unpopular or offensive to many people.

FREEDOM FORUM

FREE PRESS, FREE SPEECH, FREE SPIRIT

Censorship of Printed Materials

The censorship of printed materials—not just the press, but books, magazines, and pamphlets as well—is still as vital an issue as is freedom of speech. Before the invention of printing in the fifteenth century, books had to be produced one at a time, by hand. But the printing press allowed books to be manufactured in large numbers, and they gradually became a major way to spread ideas.

The Banning of Books

Books have always been a threat to dictators and governments that want to keep people from knowing the truth or from learning different points of view. In the twentieth century, all kinds of governments have banned

In 1989, author Salman Rushdie's life was threatened because the Muslim government was offended by the contents of his book, *The Satanic Verses.*

books to prevent people from learning about ideas that the government feels are threatening.

On May 10, 1933, the Nazi government in Germany staged a symbolic public burning of books it had banned. The works of such writers as Sigmund Freud, Karl Marx, and Thomas Mann, along with hundreds of others, were tossed into a huge bonfire. For the twelve years the Nazis ruled Germany (1933–1945), the works of the major thinkers of Western civilization were banned from schools and libraries. In their place were left the few writers approved as "safe" for the German people to read.

A more recent example of an attack on printed material—and on writers—occurred in 1989. Salman Rushdie, a Muslim writer living in Great Britain, published a novel called *The Satanic*

In 1933, freedom of the press was obliterated as the Nazi government burned more than 20,000 books it did not approve of.

Verses, in which the prophet Muhammad, the founder of the Muslim religion, was a character. Within weeks of the novel's publication, the Muslim government of Iran declared that Rushdie had insulted the name of Muhammad. They offered a $1-million reward to anyone who would kill Rushdie as a punishment for the way he had portrayed Muhammad in his novel.

Rushdie went into hiding under the protection of the British government in order to avoid assassination. Worldwide, the publishing community rallied to his side. On a number of occasions since then, Rushdie has been an unannounced speaker at publishing conferences, where he has given speeches that strongly support the rights of writers to publish their works without interference from governments. In actuality, the order to kill him is still in force, and Rushdie lives in hiding.

Although not as dramatic as the Rushdie case, groups in the United States still attempt to ban books despite the long tradition of freedom of the press. Some African-Americans, for example, are sharply critical of the classic novel *Huckleberry Finn*, by Mark Twain. They believe it is a racist book and should not be taught in school or even be on library shelves. Attacks against specific books have always been a feature of censorship struggles within the United States.

Who Controls
What Is in a Textbook?
Textbooks may seem an unusual arena for the issues of censorship. After all, aren't the books in your classroom supposed to be objective and free of bias?

In fact, some of the fiercest battles about censorship in recent years have occurred over textbooks. Unlike the examples of government censorship in Nazi Germany and Iran, the content of textbooks has been challenged by many different people and groups representing clashing points of view.

Science textbooks, for example, became an arena for the battle over the teaching of evolution. Some Christian fundamentalist groups believe that the Bible's account of God's creation of the world is true as written—namely, that God created the earth and human beings in seven days. They oppose the concept of evolution, which was proposed in the nineteenth century by the naturalist Charles Darwin.

Although most of the scientific community no longer disputes evolution, religious groups opposing it do not want it to appear in textbooks as "fact." Instead, they demand that the biblical account, which they call "creationism," be included in textbooks as a legitimate alternative. Their campaigns have been successful in several states, including Tennessee, Texas, and California, where textbooks are required to include creationism.

Charles Darwin believed that all animals, including human beings, evolved gradually over millions of years.

In Texas, Mel and Norma Gabler have spent twenty-five years criticizing textbooks on all sorts of grounds. The Gablers oppose the teaching of the "new math." They believe that because 1+1 does not always equal 2 in the new math, it teaches that there are "no absolutes," a concept they feel will confuse students who will then become extremely frustrated and "turn to crime and drugs." They have created an industry devoted to examining textbooks being considered for use in Texas, and they appear at public hearings to make their views known. Opponents of people like the Gablers see their pressure as just another form of censorship.

Another ongoing textbook fight has been over "multiculturalism." Until recent years, textbooks told mainly the story of white men in America. The contributions of women, nonwhites, and immigrants were not told as fully, or were not mentioned at all. During the 1980s, under pressure from peoples whose history had been neglected, textbook publishers began to make their books "multicultural," covering the many cultures that make up the history of the United States.

Opponents of multiculturalism in schoolbooks maintain that it is a subtle form of censorship. They believe that people who support multiculturalism are being "politically correct" and are demanding that history be told only from a multicultural point of

This 1992 demonstration against school policy in New York City was attended by people who were against teaching multiculturalism in schools because they felt it was a form of censorship.

view. This criticism was exactly the same one made against the older versions of textbooks, which tended to focus on white men and white political leaders.

Local Community Standards

The books available to you in the public library depend to some extent on where you live. The United States has a long tradition of allowing local communities to determine their own standards of morality and behavior. Public libraries use taxpayers' money to purchase books for the general public. If one group of people objects to a certain kind of book being on a public library's shelves, the group has the right to demand that the book be removed. For those who believe in a complete and open exchange of ideas, this kind of behavior is nothing more than censorship.

In the 1930s, the writings of novelist Henry Miller were banned from most states in the country. Miller often described sexual situations in graphic detail and used four-letter words in doing so. Today, Miller's works appear in libraries all over the country and are taught in college literature courses.

Although standards may have changed, some modern writers face similar problems. For example, the writer Judy Blume has found her books under attack. Blume's books, including *Are You*

Book Banning in Queens: Family Values or Censorship?

The public schools in New York City teach about one million children. This huge school system is made up of many different cultural heritages, races, and religions.

Books used in schools try to reflect this diversity and teach respect for our multicultural heritage. But certain books create controversy because of their subject matter.

In 1994, in Queens, New York, a school-board member named Frank Borzellieri tried to ban books he felt were "anti-American." One was called *I Hate English*, by Ellen Levine. In this book, Levine describes the difficulties a young Chinese girl has in learning English. Borzellieri believed the book was anti-American because it encouraged children to feel separate from American society and didn't encourage them to learn English.

Another book he wanted banned was *Young Martin's Promise*, by Alex Haley, a children's biography of the late civil rights leader Dr. Martin Luther King, Jr. Borzellieri claimed that it failed to tell the "truth" about King. He was "a leftist hoodlum with significant communist ties," Borzellieri said.

The news spread quickly of Borzellieri's book-banning campaign, and publishers, writers, librarians, teachers, and others opposed to censorship flocked to a public hearing. Before the hearing began, however, Borzellieri was removed as head of the school board's curriculum committee. The hearing went on, with speakers attacking censorship and defending the rights of children to learn about our multicultural heritage.

Although very few people could defend Borzellieri's position, efforts to ban books from schools go on throughout the country. Should moral values be taught in school? If so, whose values?

There God? It's Me, Margaret?, deal with the many difficulties of growing up, as well as problems of friendship and sex. Their subject matter offended people, including religious fundamentalists, who wanted them banned from school libraries.

Censoring Student Newspapers: Fair or Unfair?

Perhaps your school publishes a newspaper that is run by and for the students. Do you have the right to publish anything in such a newspaper? Or can you be censored? Do you, as a student, have rights under the First Amendment?

This issue came before the Supreme Court in 1988, in a case called *Hazelwood School District v. Kuhlmeier.* High school students in St. Louis, Missouri, published a newspaper called *Spectrum.* In a 1983 issue, they published two stories the principal didn't like. One was on the effects of divorce on students, and the other about three pregnant students.

The principal objected to the divorce story because a girl was quoted criticizing her father. And although the pregnant students were not mentioned by name, they could be identified. The principal ordered that the stories be dropped.

Members of the *Spectrum* staff sued, charging a violation of their First Amendment rights. By a 5 to 3 decision, the Court justices held that the principal had a right to suppress the stories because a student paper is not a "public forum" and that school officials had the right to "impose reasonable restrictions on student speech." Three justices were opposed. They maintained that school officials must allow student expression, even if it interferes with educational purposes. This decision showed that students do not have the full range of protected speech within school. Outside of school, however, they do.

A Reporter's Sources: Should They Be Confidential?

One of the ways reporters gather information for their stories is through the use of confidential sources. They rely on information from people who promise to give it—on the condition their names not be revealed.

State and local governments have challenged reporters in court trials, demanding they reveal their sources so the government can prosecute criminals. Most reporters have refused, and a number have gone to jail rather than reveal their sources.

Reporters believe that if they cannot promise people confidentiality, they will lose their sources. This would be a kind of censorship. But many judges and prosecutors believe the right to protect a source is not as strong as the need to prosecute criminals. If a reporter's information is vital to convict, it cannot be withheld from a court.

5

Censorship of the Arts

The invention of movies and television in the twentieth century brought up new issues in the ongoing debate over censorship. The framers of the Constitution lived in a world in which ideas were passed mainly by the spoken word and through print. The wording of the First Amendment reflects the time in which it was written. *Speech* and the *press* were the only ways that people communicated ideas.

But modern inventions created new ways to communicate and, therefore, new challenges to First Amendment freedoms. This chapter examines censorship in the movies, on television, and in popular music.

In the early days of movies, gangster scenes were rarely bloody and romance took the place of sex. The movie industry censored itself, so not to risk losing its audience.

The Movies: Self-Censorship in Search of Profit?

The movie industry became a big success in America after 1910. With the invention of motion pictures, a new art form developed—and one that Americans loved. The number of American moviegoers grew steadily as people flocked by the millions to see such stars as Charlie Chaplin, Rudolph Valentino, and Gloria Swanson.

Early movies were silent. But in 1927, the first spoken dialogue was used in a film called *The Jazz Singer*, starring Al Jolson. By then, the movie industry was profitable enough to be concerned about holding its audience—which meant making films for the largest number of people and not doing anything to offend the moviegoing public.

In 1922, the Motion Picture Producers and Distributors of America was founded by William H. Hays. This organization, which later became the Motion Picture Association of America, established a code to make sure that all movies produced in America followed certain moral standards. Foul language, nudity, the use of words that had sexual overtones to them (*breast*, for example), and the depiction of various forms of sexuality and violence—were all banned from films. And they were banned voluntarily by the moviemakers. These rules, unofficially called the "Hays Code," governed the movie industry for some thirty years.

Some people believed that the Hays Code worked to suppress true creativity. Look at any film that was made in the 1930s and compare it to what you see on the screen today. In 1930s movies, there was romance—not sex. Couples only kissed on screen. Gangsters in early movies were gunned down, and cowboys and Indians fought each other, but the moviegoing public never saw a lot of blood.

By the 1960s times had changed, and audiences were more willing to view the kinds of things that had been banned by the Hays Code. In 1966, the Hays Code was officially dropped, and in 1968, a voluntary, industry-wide classification system replaced it. It was called the Motion Picture Code and Rating Program, and was created in part to avoid a government-regulated system.

Under the new code, moviemakers would voluntarily give their movies one of four general ratings: "G" for general audience, all ages admitted; "PG" for parental guidance suggested; "R" for restricted audience, with no one under 17 admitted unless accompanied by an adult; and "X" for no one under 17 admitted at all. Specific age limits are allowed to be adjusted by individual state laws. For example, some states have added age requirements to the "PG" classification (PG-13 or PG-17). Before seeing a film, a moviegoer may check its rating and decide whether to see it, or allow a child to see it.

William Hays was responsible for the Hays Code, the first unofficial rules that guided what was and was not appropriate to show in movies.

Does the Movie Rating System Work?

Is the movie rating system a legitimate means of describing the content of movies? Or is it a form of censorship?

These questions have no easy answers, especially when one examines how the ratings are applied. Extremely violent movies, for example, will often have only an "R" rating, whereas movies with sexual content but no violence may wind up with an "X" rating. In the summer of 1994, a movie opened called *Natural Born Killers*, starring Woody Harrelson and Juliette Lewis. *Natural Born Killers* is the story of a young couple who go on a murderous rampage. In the course of the movie, fifty-two people die violent deaths. The mother of the character played by Juliette Lewis is set on fire, her father is drowned, and diners in a coffee shop are mowed down by gunfire. The film received an "R" rating, which means that children under seventeen may see it if accompanied by a parent.

Why, some people ask, is a movie like this not rated "X"? Many people believe that there is a direct relationship between TV and movie violence and violence that occurs in real life. Although psychologists and sociologists disagree about whether film and TV violence lead to real violence, the success of a movie like *Natural Born Killers* raises questions about the values of our society and about the purpose of the movie rating system. Most movie producers do not want an "X" rating because it keeps away a large portion of the moviegoing public—young people. Because violence alone is never enough to get an "X" rating, moviemakers have less fear about using violence in their films.

Hollywood does not seem ready to change the rating system, but many people believe that it represents a double standard that rewards violence and punishes sexual themes. It is a form of self-censorship not in the name of morality, but of profits.

Censorship and Television

Television came of age in the 1950s as millions of Americans got their first TV sets and enjoyed such popular shows as "I Love Lucy" and, later, "Father Knows Best." Unlike the movies, television was regulated by the government because it is transmitted over the airwaves, which fall under the jurisdiction of the Federal Communications Commission (FCC). Because there are only a limited number of frequencies that can be used for broadcasting, the FCC controls the rights to use them by issuing licenses to TV stations.

Under the law, these licenses must be renewed every three years. When a TV station's license is up for renewal, the FCC reviews the station's "overall performance." Although the FCC's regulations

Early television shows censored themselves in much the same way as the movies did. "I Love Lucy," for example, was clean comedy that never covered material that would disturb its audience.

forbid censorship of the content of TV programs, the fact that a station is under review by the government may have an affect on what it broadcasts. License-review procedures used by the FCC may act as a form of censorship by making TV stations alter programs out of fear of government regulators.

TV shows from the 1950s are similar to the early movies. Lucy and Ricky Ricardo on "I Love Lucy" never used foul language, never had any arguments that were anything but funny to the audience, and never referred to anything having to do with sex. Much more violence and sex is tolerated today, but network TV (television sent over the public airwaves) still shies away from full frontal nudity, most foul language, and extreme forms of violence. When a movie is shown on network TV, violence and sexual situations are either deleted or are dubbed with less offensive dialogue. There are also shows that are preceded by a warning message, alerting viewers that the program may contain violence or some partial nudity.

Like moviemakers, TV producers are sensitive to the likes and dislikes of their audience. For example, a TV show with "adult" themes is more likely to be broadcast after 9:00 P.M., when children are supposedly asleep and not watching TV.

The Cable TV
Challenge
The spread of cable TV in the 1980s and early 1990s, has brought the issue of censorship of television once more before the public. Unlike network television, which is transmitted over public airwaves, cable TV is transmitted on private cables. Cable TV companies are privately run and people subscribe and pay monthly fees to the cable company. The only way you can get cable TV is by inviting it into your home. As such, cable TV has not been subjected to the same rules and regulations of network TV.

Cable channels offer a wide variety of programming, including shows that would never be seen on network TV. Programs depicting sexual situations, nudity, strong language, and controversial material are shown on many cable channels. Does this mean that cable TV is beyond the reach of censorship? No. Local community standards, as is the case with books, speech, and the movies, are applied on cable companies. Since there are so many cable companies, a customer has the choice of switching.

The impact of consumer pressure can be seen in the case of a cartoon show called "Beavis and Butthead." This cable TV show, which appeared on MTV, upset many parents in 1993, because the characters, Beavis and Butthead, set fire to things, attacked each other, and laughed at violence and the pain of others. The controversy intensified when a child who had watched the program set fire to his home. Opponents of the show claimed the youngster was imitating "Beavis and Butthead." The protests drew the attention of some government officials, and MTV took action to quiet the controversy. Instead of canceling the program, however, the cable network merely moved it to a later time period when children were presumably asleep.

"Beavis and Butthead" may never have made it on network television, but it proved very popular on cable TV, where no licenses need to be renewed by the FCC. Nevertheless, pressure from individuals and communities was felt strongly enough for the cable companies to respond. Is this censorship? Some people believe it is, pointing out that those who do not want to look at programs like "Beavis and Butthead" should simply get up and turn off the TV or switch to another channel. Others, however,

believe that community standards should apply to cable TV just as they do to material that appears in print or that is on the networks.

The violent antics of "Beavis and Butthead" led MTV to submit to partial censorship by rescheduling the time slot.

Popular Music and Censorship

Mary Elizabeth (Tipper) Gore, the wife of then-Senator Albert Gore, Jr., was concerned about the lyrics of some of the popular rap music. They were lyrics, she believed, that advocated violence against women and that put down homosexuals. They showed no dignity for people and—in her view—were harmful because they encouraged hatred and intolerance.

Tipper Gore believed that buyers should be warned in advance about their contents. Joining

Tipper Gore led a campaign for warning labels to be placed on music that contains "harmful" material.

forces with others, she began to pressure record companies to put warning labels on records stating that the content may be offensive to some people.

The campaign to label records provoked an intense debate. Although Tipper Gore denied she was trying to censor recordings, some people believed her campaign would do just that. If artists were afraid that people were looking over their shoulders as they wrote music, they would not be enjoying the freedoms necessary to create.

Gore's campaign for record labels led to the industry voluntarily applying a rating system that is in effect today. Opponents believed that Gore, and groups of other prominent people, had used their influence to pressure the industry to cave in to their demands. In other words, they had censored free artistic expression in the name of their own personal views. Gore's supporters, however, believed that record companies needed to act responsibly toward the public and warn them about offensive material. (Some supporters were African-American women who were upset because many rap artists are African-American and these women felt some of the artists were doing a disservice to their race.)

Is the self-censorship described in movies and in the case of song lyrics an attack on First Amendment freedoms? Or is it good business aimed at giving the majority of people what they want?

2 Live Crew: Should Song Lyrics Be Censored?

Local communities in Florida have some of the strictest laws in the country concerning obscenity. Because of local community pressure, judges are likely to enforce those laws.

In June 1990, a judge in Fort Lauderdale ruled that a record album by the rap group 2 Live Crew was obscene. The album, *As Nasty As They Wanna Be*, contained lyrics that used foul language and spoke of sex and violence. Many people were upset by lyrics that seemed to advocate violence against women.

A judge ruled that the album had no serious artistic merit and did not fall under the protection of the First Amendment. This guideline had been approved by the Supreme Court, and the judge believed his ruling did not violate the First Amendment.

Shortly after the ruling, a record-store owner near Fort Lauderdale was arrested for selling *As Nasty As They Wanna Be* to an undercover police officer. The following evening, two singers in the 2 Live Crew group were arrested for performing the banned lyrics at a concert in nearby Hollywood, Florida.

The record-store owner was convicted of selling obscene material and received a fine. But at a separate trial, the 2 Live Crew singers were found not guilty. In this case, the jury believed that their song had to be considered artistic expression. The jury also felt that the concert was in the same category as a political rally and could not be stopped by the police.

The opposition to certain lyrics has created alliances among people who have often been enemies on other issues. Some conservative groups were supported by liberal groups who also objected to the content. On the other side were liberal groups, like the American Civil Liberties Union (ACLU) that objects to any form of censorship, which had the support of conservative businesspeople in the record industry. These people were afraid that censorship would hurt their business.

Another issue was whether lyrics that speak of violence can lead to violence. Should the government be allowed to censor the lyrics of popular music because people object to the content, or because they might lead to violence?

Luther Campbell, of 2 Live Crew, gestures in protest during a 1990 espisode of the "Donahue" show.

Censorship in the Computer Age

As we have seen in the previous chapters, advances in technology create opportunities for the spread of ideas and information, as well as new dangers of censorship. As we approach the end of the twentieth century, the computer has opened new ways to share information and ideas. Instead of waiting for something to travel by old-fashioned mail, we can now send documents by electronic mail (E-mail) or by fax. Or, we may have a conversation via our computer with someone thousands of miles away. Other new technology also allows us to share information in record time. For example,

Censorship, particularly of material adults feel is not suitable for young people, has become increasingly difficult in this age of computers.

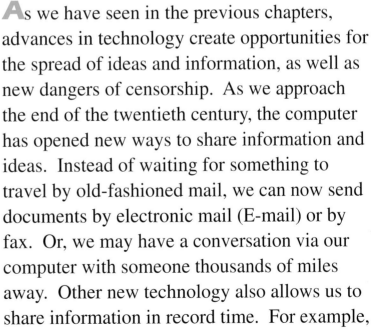

audio and videocassettes make it possible for us to make and share with others our own recordings and videotapes.

Is censorship dead because of new technology? Old kinds of censorship are harder to enforce because of computers, faxes, and other technology. Book banning becomes almost impossible when one can transmit books by fax or E-mail, or when books can be produced on personal computers. Attempts by authorities to prevent someone from speaking to a large number of people are made more difficult when a small audiocassette can be copied over and over and handed from one person to another.

But new and different kinds of censorship issues arise in the age of the computer. The most important focuses on the issue of privacy.

Computers
Versus Privacy
Almost everything seems to be computerized these days. Computers are in our schools and homes and in almost every type of business. Many of our daily activities wind up being tracked on a computer. Things we buy— groceries, clothing, books, or hamburgers—are rung up on computers. Records of our bank statements are kept in large computers. Letters and work we do for school may be written on a computer and even sent by E-mail or fax to friends.

The price we pay for this fast technology is a loss of privacy. Computers can be linked into "networks." For example, supermarket purchases are rung up on the supermarket's computer and stored there. It is a kind of record of what you buy. That information can be made available—for a fee—to another company that wants to sell you some other kind of product.

Bank records are another example. All of the information about people's money—how much they have, how much they deposit or withdraw—is made available to the Internal Revenue Service (IRS), the

E-mail and Censorship

On-line computer services and the use of E-mail is a good example of how privacy and censorship are linked. On-line services like Prodigy, CompuServe, and America Online are private networks that offer a variety of services for a fee. One of the most popular of their features is E-mail. Anyone who belongs to an on-line service can log on, enter a "chat room," and talk live, via computer, to others who are on-line at the same time. These conversations are supposed to be private— between you and the other person or persons. But before long you may notice that on-line services have "guides"—people who quietly check on what is being talked about in the chat rooms. If the guide discovers something that is objectionable or even possibly illegal, he or she will interrupt your conversation and warn you to stop.

What do on-line computer services object to? Most do not let you use the service to actively sell any product or service. All on-line services forbid the use of foul language, being abusive to others on-line, and soliciting for sexual purposes. These are understandable rules, because on-line services must abide by the laws of the states they operate in and the federal government. Nevertheless, you are still being watched and possibly censored. When you are on-line, you have limited free speech and you really have no privacy at all. Even if a guide never sees what you've typed, the information still becomes part of the on-line service's computer data bank.

tax-collecting agency of the government. This information is to make sure people aren't cheating on their taxes.

Because of computer networks, information about people and what they do can be shared—without their knowledge. All kinds of information about people and their habits is spread via the "information superhighway"—the networks of computer data banks in private industry and in government. But is this a censorship issue or merely a privacy issue? Both, and the two are linked.

What the Government Knows About You

Because computers can store unlimited amounts of information—and because they are linked through networks—the government assembles a lot of information about people. The IRS has a record of everyone's tax history. What else is likely to be in government computers? Tickets people get for driving or parking violations are stored in government computers. A person's political affiliation is probably knowledge available to the government, too, especially if that person is a regular voter or has signed any petitions. And, as we have seen, someone's history as a consumer is already in many different computer networks and probably ends up in one government computer network or another.

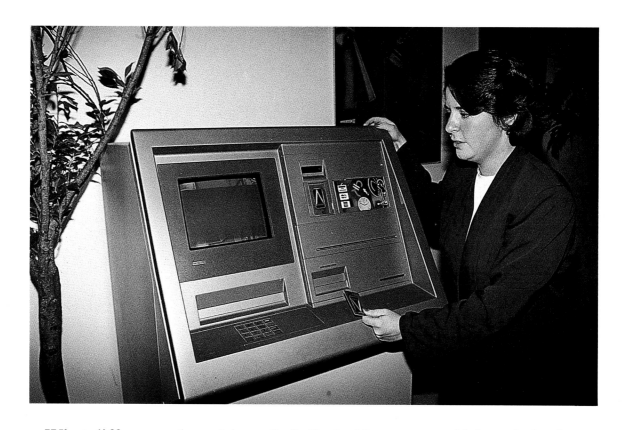

What difference does this make? Probably not much as long as we have First Amendment rights that are still protected. But many people are concerned that all this information in the hands of the government can be used to censor our activities as a free people. And it is almost impossible to get your name removed from a computer data bank once it's in. Every time someone uses an ATM card at a bank, pays taxes, or buys something with a credit card, information about that person is entered into a data bank. And that information can be shared with the local, state, and federal governments.

Modern technology has decreased our right to privacy. Simply using an ATM allows the government access to personal information.

The Fax and Censorship

"Fax" is shorthand for facsimile. This technology uses telephone lines to transmit words and pictures. A fax machine is plugged into a telephone line. By feeding paper documents into it, you can transmit them to another fax machine. You may also fax documents directly from your computer by use of a modem, a device that hooks your computer to a phone line. Faxes may also be sent from one computer to another without the use of a special fax machine. Almost all businesses have fax machines, and increasing numbers of private individuals are faxing from their home computers or fax machines.

The invention of the fax was a major blow to censorship. Unlike on-line services, which can be monitored, faxes offer a maximum degree of privacy and therefore are almost impossible to censor. In fact, the fax machine played a significant role in the downfall of communism in Eastern Europe in 1989, and in the Soviet Union in 1991.

Fax technology has made it nearly impossible for a government to censor the information that people exchange with one another.

The Communist governments in these countries had always used censorship of speech and printed materials to maintain their power and to control information. But technology proved to be their worst enemy. When they tried to jam radio broadcasts from Western Europe or the United States, people simply got hold of recordings of them on audiocassettes and passed them around to whomever wanted to listen. They tried to ban books, but then came the invention of the photocopying machine. The Soviet authorities were so afraid of these machines that they prohibited anyone from having one unless the government approved. And almost no one ever got permission. Illegal ownership of a photocopying machine was punishable by long prison terms.

But the fax machine was the most severe blow to Communist censorship, because it allowed unmonitored information to come in from the outside through a simple phone call. Communist newspapers told of world events from a Communist perspective. But anyone with a fax machine simply had to ask a friend in the West to fax a daily newspaper, which could then be shared with people who did not have fax machines.

During the final years of Communist rule in Eastern Europe and the Soviet Union, censorship of information became increasingly more difficult, in large part because of the technology of the age of the computer. With the control of information slipping away, the governments of these countries could no longer exercise the same amount of control over what people heard or read as they had in the past.

**Protecting Our Freedoms
in the Computer Age** The founders of our
country believed that the best way to guarantee
freedom was by protecting free speech and a free
press. For all of the fears about government and
private snooping, the computer and new technology
can also be used to protect our freedoms. For example, many on-line computer services allow you to
E-mail the White House. By simply entering your
thoughts and ideas and pressing a button, you can
mail a letter to the president instantly. Because of
the computer, the president and his staff can communicate immediately with the public and make
their views known to each other.

   The home computer allows us to publish pamphlets and even books, and fax and E-mail them to a
large number of people. Computers are being used
more and more, and the kinds of challenges they
will present to our First Amendment freedoms are
still unknown. But a free society has a better
chance of remaining free as long as information is
shared. For all its unknown dangers, the computer
may also be used to protect our freedom of speech
and the press.

Glossary

book banning The attempt by individuals, groups, or the government to prevent certain books from being read by others.

cable TV TV transmission over private cable lines.

censorship The limiting or prevention of free speech or a free press by individuals, groups, or the government.

commercial speech A legal term for advertising, a kind of speech that is not protected by the First Amendment.

community standards A term used to describe the kind of morality supported by the majority of the people in a community.

E-mail Electronic mail, sent by means of a computer to another computer.

fax Short for "facsimile," a technology that allows documents or pictures to be transmitted via telephone lines.

Federal Communications Commission (FCC) A government agency responsible for issuing licenses to TV networks that use the public airwaves for broadcasting.

fighting words Speech that deliberately attempts to incite violence.

First Amendment The constitutional guarantee adopted in 1791 for the protection of freedom of speech, press, and religion.

libel A false statement or a statement that is damaging to someone's character that appears in print or on television.

Motion Picture Code and Rating System A code that the movie industry uses to rate its films in order to warn the audience about the content and appropriate age level of the audience.

obscenity Sexual or otherwise offensive printed material or speech determined to have no significant social or artistic value by community standards.

prior restraint Stopping publication of a book, newspaper, or magazine article before it is published.

Sedition Act A law passed in 1798 making it a crime to criticize the U.S. government.

slander Speech that damages a person's character or reputation.

For Further Reading

Evans, J. Edward. *Freedom of the Press.* Minneapolis, Minn.: Lerner, 1990.

Hentoff, Nat. *The First Freedom: The Tumultuous History of Free Speech in America.* New York: Delacorte Press, 1988.

Lang, Susan B., and Paul Lang. *Censorship.* New York: Franklin Watts, 1993.

Pascoe, Elaine. *Freedom of Expression: The Right to Speak Out in America.* Brookfield, Conn: Millbrook Press, 1992.

Steele, Philip. *Censorship.* New York: New Discovery Books, 1992.

Trager, Oliver. *The Arts & Media in America: Freedom or Censorship?* New York: Facts On File, 1991.

Source Notes

"Group School Censorship Rises." *New York Times,* August 31, 1994, as reprinted in America Online computer download service.

Lang, Susan B., and Paul Lang. *Censorship.* New York: Franklin Watts, 1993.

Leeson, Susan M., and James C. Foster. *Constitutional Law: Cases in Context.* New York: St. Martin's Press, 1992.

Pareles, Jon. "A Rap Group's Lyrics Venture Close to the Edge of Obscenity." *New York Times,* June 14, 1990.

Pascoe, Elaine. *Freedom of Expression: The Right to Speak Out in America.* Brookfield, Conn.: Millbrook Press, 1992.

Russo, Francine. "Welcome to the Jungle." *Entertainment Weekly,* September 9, 1994.

Small, William J. *Political Power and the Press.* New York: Norton, 1972.

Wayne, Stephen J., et al. *The Politics of American Government: Foundations, Participation, Institutions, and Policy.* New York: St. Martin's Press, 1994.

Index